THE GIRL WHO LOST THE LIGHT IN HER EYES

This beautifully illustrated and sensitively written storybook has been created to be used therapeutically with children experiencing loss. Telling the story of a young girl who searches high and low for the light that is missing from her eyes, it encourages the child to move through the grieving process in order to find colour in the world again. The colourful illustrations and engaging story are designed to inspire conversation around loss, and will help develop emotional literacy and resilience in children and young people.

This book is also available to purchase alongside a pocket guidebook as part of the two-component set, *Supporting Children and Young People Who Experience Loss*. The full set includes:

- *The Girl Who Lost the Light in Her Eyes,* a colourfully illustrated and sensitively written storybook, designed to encourage conversation and support emotional literacy.

- *Using the Expressive Arts with Children and Young People Who Experience Loss*, a supporting guidebook that explores a relational approach and promotes creative expression as a way through loss or bereavement.

Perfectly crafted to spark communication around a difficult topic, this is an invaluable tool for practitioners, educators, parents, and anybody else looking to support a child or young person through loss or bereavement.

Juliette Ttofa is a specialist educational psychologist with a long-standing interest in the complex issues surrounding trauma, attachment needs and emotional resilience.

She specialises in supporting children and young people, their schools and families in understanding and responding to social, emotional and mental health needs through training, therapeutic support, and assessment and consultancy.

She is a Registered Sandplay Therapist and is passionate about using the expressive arts to support the mental health and wellbeing of all children and young people.

The Girl Who Lost the Light in Her Eyes

Written by
Juliette Ttofa

Illustrated by
Paul Greenhouse

Routledge
Taylor & Francis Group
LONDON AND NEW YORK

First published 2021
by Routledge
2 Park Square, Milton Park, Abingdon, Oxon OX14 4RN

and by Routledge
52 Vanderbilt Avenue, New York, NY 10017

Routledge is an imprint of the Taylor & Francis Group, an informa business

© 2021 Juliette Ttofa
Illustrations © 2021 Paul Greenhouse

British Library Cataloguing-in-Publication Data
A catalogue record for this book is available from the British Library

Library of Congress Cataloging-in-Publication Data
Names: Ttofa, Juliette, author. | Greenhouse, Paul (Paul Michael), illustrator.
Title: The girl who lost the light in her eyes : an illustrated storybook / Juliette Ttofa ; illustrated by Paul Greenhouse.
Description: Abington, Oxon ; New York, NY : Routledge, 2020. | Summary: A girl searches high and low for the light that is missing from her eyes.
Identifiers: LCCN 2020012780 (print) | LCCN 2020012781 (ebook) | ISBN 9780367524418 (pbk) | ISBN 9781003057987 (ebk)
Subjects: CYAC: Grief—Fiction. | Loss (Psychology)—Fiction. | Resilience (Personality trait)—Fiction.
Classification: LCC PZ7.1.T8 Gk 2020 (print) | LCC PZ7.1.T8 (ebook) | DDC [E]—dc23
LC record available at https://lccn.loc.gov/2020012780
LC ebook record available at https://lccn.loc.gov/2020012781

ISBN: 978-0-367-52441-8 (pbk)
ISBN: 978-1-003-05798-7 (ebk)

Typeset in Calibri
by Apex CoVantage, LLC

For AP & EP with love

There was once a girl
who lost the light in her eyes…

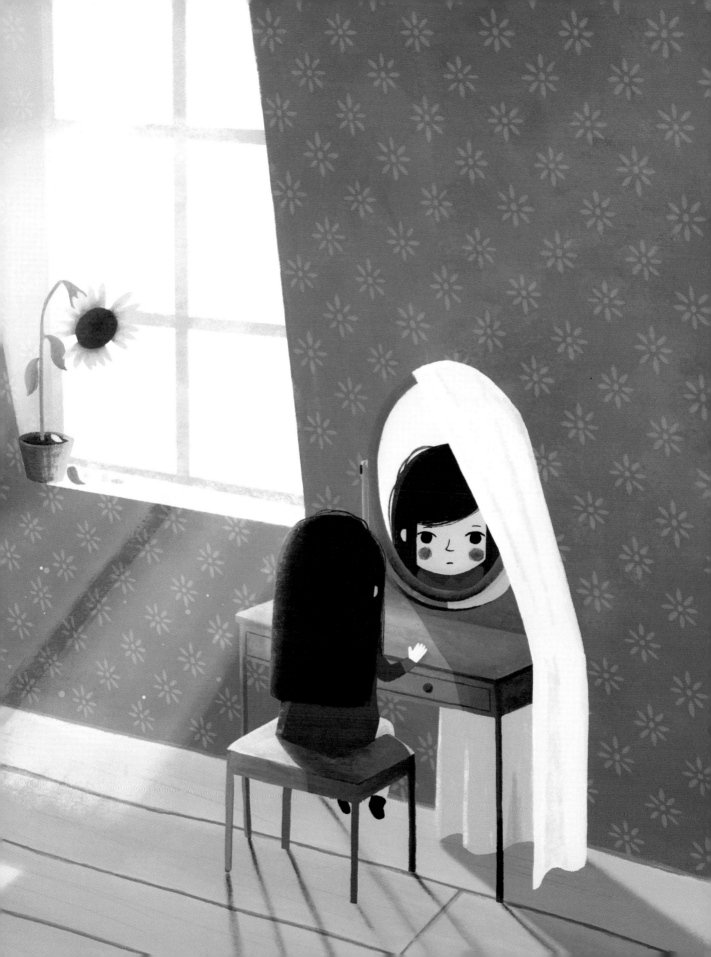

She searched and searched for it high and low.
Under the shallow, babbling brook
that flowed like laughter through her town.

Inside the sparkling drops of dew,
that glistened like a smile
upon the blades of grass.

Through the fresh-scented pine trees,
that waved hello
in the forests.

And amongst the twinkling stars that flickered
like fairy lights high above the rooftops…

But find the light from her eyes *she could not*.

The beautiful world turned dark
and drained of all its colour.
The girl's face turned an ashen-grey.
And she became so very sad…

As if in a dream, the fireflies of the night carried her off to a faraway place.

They covered her with moss and leaves and petals.
And there she slept…

When she awoke,
the forest animals had gathered around her.
"Where am I?" enquired the girl.
But there came no answer.

Only a soft humming sound, which she followed curiously through the trees.

Until she saw him: the painter boy.
Humming a tune to himself.
And painting colour back into the world.

"Can you paint the light back into my eyes?"
she asked the boy hopefully.
The boy put down his paintbrush gently.

"The light in one's eyes is difficult to paint,"
he replied softly.
And the girl's shoulders sank.

"You don't paint it, you see," he explained.
"In fact, you only outline the light that is already there."

And then he said:

*"The light of your eyes never leaves you.
It is only that it becomes covered by the darkness."*

So, as delicately as he could,
he dipped his paintbrush
into the ink-black wells of the girl's eyes
and began to paint tear drops.

Cool, salty tears that spilled out and rolled like a river
down her face.

Tears
that told the
story of her
sadness.

A
painful
story, told over
many days, that the
boy watched unfold
before his own
eyes,

and felt
deeply in
his heart.

Until
one day,
the girl cried
no more.

And then he noticed it.
Shining like a light at the end of a dark tunnel:
the tiny sparkle of light that had caught in the girl's eye.

And little by little,
it illuminated the colour in the world
once more.